ARABIA
AND
THE GULF

ARABIA
AND
THE GULF:
IN ORIGINAL PHOTOGRAPHS
1880-1950

BY
ANDREW WHEATCROFT

KEGAN PAUL INTERNATIONAL
LONDON, BOSTON, MELBOURNE
AND HENLEY

First published in 1982 by Kegan Paul International Ltd
39 Store Street, London WC1E 7DD,
9 Park Street, Boston, Mass. 02108, USA;
296 Beaconsfield Parade, Middle Park,
Melbourne, 3206, Australia and
Broadway House, Newtown Road,
Henley-on-Thames, Oxon RG9 1EN
Set in 14pt Bembo
and printed in Great Britain by
BAS Printers Limited, Over Wallop, Hampshire
Text © The Wessell Press 1982
This selection of photographs © The Wessell Press 1982

Library of Congress Cataloguing in Publication Data

Main entry under title:

Arabia in original photographs, 1880–1950.

Includes bibliographical references.
1. Arabia – Description and travel – Views.
I. Wheatcroft, Andrew.
DS204.2.A73   953'.04   81-18615

ISBN 0-7103-0016-6   AACR2

For my children
James
Artemis
Thomas
Anneyce

CONTENTS

FOREWORD

The art of photography is now an immensely popular hobby throughout the world. However, when it first started it was available only to a very few people who had the money and determination to indulge in this activity. Then as now, each photograph is a reflection of the interests and tastes of the photographer, be he amateur or professional.

The present book is not just a collection of photographs but rather an illustrated historical record. In other words it is a chronicle which is brought dramatically to life by the photographs. As its title indicates the book deals with a region about which very little was known in the West during the nineteenth and early twentieth century. It covers the region not only geographically but also sociologically and over a fairly long period of time. It spans the region from the heart of Arabia, through Western Arabia (Jeddah, Mecca and Medina), Yemen, Oman and the Gulf. It depicts the life of the Arab, not only rulers but also the ordinary people in their daily activities. These photographs also show the changes which have taken place over the period from 1880 to 1950, giving the reader an opportunity to link the past with the present.

It is interesting to see that many of the photographs were taken in the early days of photography and they were not taken only by Western travellers in the region but also by the Arabs themselves. One of the early Arab photographers was al-Sayyid Abd al-Ghaffār, a physician of Mecca in the 1880s. The photograph on page 123 is an example of his work.

It must have been a very difficult task choosing the photographs; writing the appropriate text to complement them must have been even more difficult. The author has provided us with a first class selection of varied and striking photographs, and a lively text to match.

The book is not only a pleasure to look at and read but is also a permanent record of people and places which, in many cases, have disappeared and gone for ever, or else have changed out of all recognition. It is of interest not only to the general reader but also to historians, anthropologists, archaeologists and ethnologists. It provides a stimulating account of the region which will provide the reader with much enjoyment and pleasure for a long time to come.

The book is also of importance at this time, when the region is the focus of increasing world-wide attention and interest.

Professor M. H. Bakalla
Curator of the Folklore Museum
King Saud University
Riyadh, Kingdom of Saudi Arabia

PREFACE

The aim of this book is not simply a nostalgic attempt to record something of the traditional life of Arabia before it vanishes, but to point up the risk to the visual record itself. In preparing this book, I have been fortunate enough to examine many collections of photographs relating to Arabia, some of which appear in these pages. They were often taken under the most arduous conditions, in the heat of the desert, and would be sent great distances – to India or Egypt, or even back to Europe – to be processed. Many of the photographs and negatives are in a poor state, and are deteriorating rapidly; within a decade, unless a concerted programme of copying and restoration is undertaken, these images will have faded beyond recall. The need for immediate action is unmistakable. All dates are given in accordance with the Gregorian calendar, save that all *hijri* dates are indicated AH.

The rendering of Arabic into English, especially with place names, poses a special difficulty. T. E. Lawrence delighted in the fact that he had spelt 'Jiddah' in numerous and mutually inconsistent ways in *The Seven Pillars of Wisdom*. I have accepted that a level of inconsistency is bound to exist but without any rejoicing. Where a writer has spelt a word in a particular fashion, I have respected his usage, even if it does not accord with modern practice. But I have used the form which is most normally understood in English today, even where a name such as 'Makkah' for Mecca is becoming more common.

ACKNOWLEDGMENTS

My gratitude extends in two directions, first towards those who have given up much of their time to discuss the matters dealt with in this book, and gently sought to correct my rash enthusiasm, and second towards those who have made available the photographs themselves. Frequently, I owe a double debt, to those many friends who have given me the background which lies behind the photographs in their possession, and then allowed me to make free with their possessions. I would wish in particular to thank Major-General James Lunt and Dr Robin Bidwell for the help and advice they have given to me, and also Mrs J. Bartosile, John Ryan Esq., Wilfred Thesiger Esq., Mrs D. C. Milne, Mrs V. P. Dickson, and Mrs B. Thomas. Others, sadly, have asked me not to acknowledge them specifically, as I would wish to. I also owe thanks to the staff of a number of corporate bodies: to the Royal Geographical Society, an earthly paradise for the researcher; to St Antony's College, Oxford, and to the Middle East Centre in the Department of Oriental Studies in the University of Cambridge, and for access to material in the possession of the University of Newcastle. The photographic library of the Hamlyn Group, and The Mansell Collection have supplied valuable material, and I am grateful for the assistance I have received from the Bildarchiv of the Osterreichische Staatsarchiv in Vienna. Avril Jordan has typed the manuscript of the book, and done much of the initial preparation of the photographs and captions. Philip de Bay and Ken Jackson have given considerable expert help in the treatment and processing of old photographs. Dr Mohammed Bakalla has given very freely both of his time and his considerable knowledge of traditional Arabia; I owe much to his help and advice. Trevor Mostyn has been good enough to read the proofs for me, though of course the usual caveat, that the remaining errors are the sole responsibility of the author, applies. Equally, I owe a great deal to Peter Hopkins for his friendship and support during the preparation of this book. Finally, to my wife, Janet, for her advice and criticism, and her insight into historic photographs, I am most thankful.

MAP
OF ARABIA

miles
0   50   100   150
0   50   100   150
kilometres

Basra •

KUWAIT

• Kuwait

Arabian Gulf

L SHAMMAR

QASIM

NEJD

Thaj •

Damman •

HASA

BAHREIN

Hofuf •

QATAR

RAS AL KHAIMAH
UMM AL QAIWAN
AJMAN
SHARJAH
DUBAI

FUJAIRAH

Gulf of Oman

Diriyyah

■ Riyadh

ABU DHABI

Buraimi
oasis

BATINA

MUSCAT

HAJAR MTS

• Muscat

SERT

•

SAUDI

JEBEL TUWAIQ

JABRIN

JEBEL AKHADAR

ARABIA

• Suleimiya

• El Hadeida

RUB'   AL - KHALI

(The Empty Quarter)

OMAN

DHOFAR
QARA MTS

• Salala

S

R

Y E M E N

HADRAMAUT

SOUTH   YEMEN

• Sana

• Mukalla

• Taiz

b el Mandeb •

Gulf of Aden

INTRODUCTION

In the spring of 1154 (AH 549) the Arab geographer al-Idrisi displayed a large silver table to his patron, King Roger II of Sicily: upon it was engraved a new map of the world. This map, and the great compilation of geographical knowledge – The Nuzhat al Mushtaq – which accompanied it had taken fifteen years to complete. It showed al-Idrisi's comprehensive knowledge of the ancient geographers, including Ptolemy (long forgotten in Europe), and the experience of generations of Arab travellers and traders, whose journeys he had culled. The map was the finest and most comprehensive of the early cosmographies. Yet, although it was produced in a noted centre of learning, indeed, one of the most replendent courts in the West, the work of al-Idrisi was forgotten.[1]

The causes for this neglect are various. Al-Idrisi stood in advance of his time, for while Europeans were content with the traditions of the *mappa mundi*, which were concerned as much with the relationship of God and man as with the concrete details of geography, he had produced a map in the more disinterested tradition of ancient science. His work was also offensive in a more particular sense. In the *mappa mundi*, Jerusalem stood at the centre of the world, with the continents ranged about the city; it was the nodal point, a junction between Earth and Heaven. In al-Idrisi's work, his map centred on Arabia, with Mecca at its core: he displayed the world-view of a Muslim rather than a Christian. Arabia was the heart of Islam, the starting point for the great movement of Islamic expansion; while political power had shifted northwards, and westwards along the coast of Africa as far as the Spanish kingdoms of al-Andalus, Arabia remained the focal point in Islam. Mecca was the *Qibla*, the direction in which every Muslim turned to pray. Even with the rediscovery of Ptolemy by the West, and the surge of European expansion by sea from the fifteenth century onwards, the Arabic tradition of trade and exploration, which had continued steadily from al-Idrisi's day, was neglected and largely ignored in the West.

Arabia remained a land of mystery, not because the land was in itself more hostile or more inclement than other regions, but because it was seen to be peripheral to European interests. When Edward Gibbon came to write his celebrated description of Arabia, he expressed the essence of Western attitudes to the peninsula:[2]

In the vacant space between Persia, Syria, Egypt, and Æthiopia, the Arabian peninsula may be conceived as a triangle of spacious but irregular dimensions. The entire surface of the peninsula exceeds in a fourfold proportion that of Germany or France; but the far greater part has been justly stigmatized with the epithets of the stony and the sandy. Even the wilds of Tartary are decked by the hand of nature with lofty trees and luxuriant herbage; and the lonesome traveller derives a sort of comfort and society from the presence of vegetable life. But in the dreary waste of Arabia, a boundless level of sand is intersected by sharp and naked mountains, and the face of the desert, without shade or shelter, is scorched by the direct and intense rays of a tropical sun. Instead of refreshing breezes, the winds, particularly from the south-west, diffuse a noxious and even deadly vapour; the hillocks of sand which they alternately raise and scatter are compared to the billows of the ocean; and whole caravans, whole armies, have been lost and buried in the whirl-wind. The common benefits of water are an object of desire and contest; and such is the scarcity of wood that some art is requisite to preserve and propagate the element of fire.

Arabia is destitute of navigable rivers, which fertilise the soil and convey its produce to the adjacent regions; the torrents that fall from the hills are imbibed by the thirsty earth; the rare and hardy plants, the tamarind or the acacia, that strike their roots into the clefts of the rocks, are nourished by the dews of the night; a scanty supply of rain is collected in cisterns and aqueducts; the wells and springs are the secret treasure of the desert; and the pilgrim of Mecca, after many a dry and sultry march, is disgusted by the taste of the waters, which have rolled over a bed of sulphur or salt. Such is the general and genuine picture of the climate of Arabia.

This 'genuine picture' was conjured up by the author in the summer-house of his garden at Lausanne, a prodigious feat of imagination. It is, perforce, fanciful, yet Gibbon presented the picture of Arabia which united all the impressions which he had culled from earlier literature with the fertility of his own imagination. And, through the enormous popularity of his *Decline and Fall of the Roman Empire*, he created a literary stereotype of *Araby*.

The Romantic notion of the Arab was a by-blow of the passion for the Noble Savage. Gibbon alludes to the 'intrepid valour' of the Arabs, and how the 'patient and active virtues of a soldier are insensibly nursed in the habits and discipline of a pastoral life.' His Danish contemporary, Carsten Niebuhr, had the advantage of having travelled in the south of Arabia; but he, too, was intoxicated by his belief in the vigour and independence of the Arab, writing that a 'Spirit of Liberty with which this warlike nation are animated, renders them incapable of servitude.' The qualities which the Romantics later took as typical of the Arab sprang from their understanding, imperfect though it was of the terrain of Arabia: only a nation of great inner strength could survive the hostility of the environment which Gibbon had described. As travellers from the West came to know the lands of Arabia at first hand, and to experience the varieties of life in the peninsula, the Romantic notions shrivelled and a new quality of admiration both for the land and its peoples emerged.

The central misunderstanding about Arabia lies in the word *desert*, defined variously as: Forsaken, Abandoned, Uninhabited, Unpeopled, Desolate, Lonely, Uncultivated and Unproductive, Barren, Waste.[3] Arabia was equated with *desert*, and thus carried with it all the string of pejoratives listed above. In fact, virtually nowhere was the country *desert* in this *absolute* sense. Colonel Pelly crossed in 1865 (AH 1284) from the Arabian Gulf to the heart of Arabia and returned to the Gulf having covered a great tract of territory:[4] each day he noted 'grass, wild flowers, and brushwood'. Even the sands of the Dahna were 'sprinkled with vegetation'. Desolation was relative, for that 'compared with the vast waste we have now crossed, even the most desert parts of Persia seem wooded and peopled, for we have seen neither tree, hut, nor fowl, and scarce a goat since we left Kuwait.' It is difficult to recognize the arid desolation of Gibbon in his description of the Nejd hills: 'Nor is there anything striking in their aspect. They are neither remarkably rugged, nor wild, nor wooded, nor watered, but rather tame in their barrenness like English Down scenery with the green peeled off.'[5] Even in the great southern desert, The Rub' al-Khali – The Empty Quarter – grazing could sometimes be found for camels, and Wilfred Thesiger's companion al-Auf described how rain would bring the desert to life:[6]

'We like winter rain best; it generally lasts longer. Summer storms, it is true, are often heavier, but the great heat at that time of year kills the seedlings, unless the rain has been heavy. However, praise be to God, rain is rain whenever it comes.' He pointed to some dead tribulus; 'Do you see that zahra? You could think it was quite dead, wouldn't you? But it's only got to rain and a month later it will be green and covered with flowers. It takes years of drought to kill these plants; they have such tremendously long roots. In a place where the plants really are dead, like the Umm al-Hait, which we saw the other day, the vegetation comes up again from seeds when at last it does rain. It does not matter how long they have lain in the sand.'

In almost every part of Arabia life was hard, dependent on the elements and the will of God. Yet this barren land sustained a few cities and many towns, a profusion of nomadic tribes, and considerable internal trade. Years after Pelly crossed from the East into central Arabia, the Austrian explorer Alois Musil travelled in northern Arabia, lived with the tribes and studied both the land

and the people with a scholarly persistence. He denied the notion of the *desert*:[7]

> Arabia is by no means the dead and death-dealing country that Caetani depicts. It is an arid region with irregular and often insufficient rainfall but after abundant rains it resembles a garden and in many places can be inhabited and tilled. That the Arabia of today is not as wealthy and populous as the Arabia of antiquity is due primarily to changes in the world's trade routes and to the lack of public security.

To appreciate the reality of Arabia rather than the qualities imposed upon it by Western convention, both literary and cultural, is the motive which lies behind this book.

The land of Arabia, in the sober language of the British Admiralty, 'resembles a broad and stout shelf sloped up sideways from east to west. The fall towards the Gulf is long and gentle, the return to the Red Sea short and steep.'[8] Along the Red Sea coast lie the provinces of the Hejaz, Asir, and the Yemen; behind them mountain, steppe and desert make communication with the interior difficult. The Hejaz was an inhospitable coast, but through its main ports Jiddah and Yambo came the flow of pilgrims to Mecca and Medina, which enriched both the rulers and the common people of the region. Before the railway was extended south from Damascus to Medina in 1908, many pilgrims travelled overland from the north in great camel convoys, as Charles Doughty had in 1876:[9]

> The new dawn appearing we removed not yet. The day risen the tents were dismantled, the camels led in ready to their companies, and halted beside their loads. We waited to hear the cannon shot which should open that year's pilgrimage. It was near ten o'clock when we heard the signal gun fired, and then, without any disorder, litters were suddenly heaved and braced upon the bearing beasts, their charges laid upon the kneeling camels and the thousands of riders, all born in the caravan countries, mounted in silence. As all is up the drivers are left standing upon their feet, or sit to rest out the latest moments on their heels: they with other camp and tent servants must ride those three hundred leagues upon their bare soles, although they faint; and are to measure the ground again upward with their weary feet from the holy places. At the second gun, fired a few moments after, the Pasha's litter advances and after him goes the head of the caravan column: another fifteen or twenty minutes we, who have places in the rear, must halt, that is until the long train is unfolded before us; then we strike our camels and the great pilgrimage is moving. There go commonly three or four camels abreast and seldom five; the length of the slow-footed multitude of men and cattle is near two miles, and the width some hundred yards in the open plains. The hajjaj were this year by their account (which may be above the truth) 6000 persons; of these more than half are serving men on foot; and 10,000 of all kinds of cattle, the most camels, then mules, hackneys, asses and a few dromedaries of

Arabians returning in security of the great convoy to their own districts. We march in an empty waste, a plain of gravel, where nothing appeared and never a road before us.

The Hejaz, with the twin holy cities of Mecca and Medina, was nominally in the hands of the Emir of Mecca, a member of a Sherifial family descended from the Prophet. But from the 1840s control rested with the Turks, and in 1886, Turkish power was increased with garrisons established in the main towns. Their influence, the annual throng of pilgrims, and the many different nationalities which made up the population of the Holy Cities, made the Hejaz different in tone from the rest of Arabia. It was also the area (apart from the coast) best known in the West, for the prohibition of the Holy Cities to non-Muslims made them a magnet to the adventurous.

While the land of the Hejaz displays a 'general barrenness relieved only by rare oases', Medina, and Taif in the mountains above Mecca, presented an impression of luxuriance and plenty. Medina, a city of some 40,000 before the First World War, was surrounded by date groves, fields and orchards: her markets were filled with bananas, limes, peaches and pomegranates in their season. Taif stands some 5,000 feet above sea-level, seventy-five miles to the south-east of Mecca. St John Philby came to the town for the first time on Christmas Day, 1917:[10]

From the top of the pass we looked down on the fair vale of Taif bathed in a dusty haze and backed by the high-reared masses of Barad and Qarnait, monster peaks of the main range silhouetted against the setting sun. . . .

The town of Taif itself is four-square, each side being roughly some 300 yards in length; formerly it was girt around by a wall of mud and stone, whose dismantled ruins contrast strangely with the neat houses and great mansions within. The central part of the town is occupied by the Suq, whose extent is out of all proportion to the needs of the permanent population, though doubtless designed with a view to accommodating the summer trade. In its rambling streets and alleys I found no system nor symmetry, the central square is of irregular shape with a mosque at the end, the Masjid al-Hadi, and the unpretentious offices and court-house of the Amir. Round the Suq to south and east are the quarters of the poorer inhabitants; to north and west are the mansions of the well-to-do. . . .

The orchards of Taif provide Mecca with quinces, pomegranates, peaches, apricots, grapes, melons, pumpkins and vegetables of many kinds; there are date-groves in the lower hamlets such as Ukhaidhar, Qaim and Marisiyya, but not at Taif itself; orange and lemon trees are found here and there, but never in profusion. In spring and early summer, when the orchards are in blossom, the valley must be lovely indeed, but in mid-winter, when I saw the trees denuded of their foliage, blossomless and sere, it must be admitted that the scene was somewhat bleak; the lofty palaces of the wealthy stood out cold and naked against a grim background of rocky ridges.

The contrast with the baking heat of Mecca or the stifling humidity of Jiddah is marked and it is a matter of no surprise that the rulers of the Hejaz, whether Turk and Sherif, or, later, Saudi princes, made Taif their summer capital. Philby was told that travel would not appeal to a citizen of Taif, 'who, placed by bountiful Providence in a veritable Paradise' with an ideal situation and a temperate climate, had little to gain by wandering in the pestilent Tihama (the coastal strip along the Red Sea) or arid deserts around.

Bountiful Providence has been kinder to Asir and the Yemen than to the Hejaz. The sandy coastal belt, the *Tihama*, extending some twenty or thirty miles deep along the Red Sea coast to the southern tip of Arabia, was less arid than the coast of the Hejaz; in the southern part of the province, the capital, Sabiya, was well irrigated and produced bountiful crops. But the *Tihama* was most famous for its livestock; and the cattle and donkeys of Asir were renowned throughout southern Arabia. In the highlands, the land was as Wilfred Thesiger described it in 1946:[11]

> There were terraced fields of wheat and barley, vines, and plots of vegetables. . . .
> Sometimes we spent the night in a castle with an Amir, sometimes in a mud cabin
> with a slave, and everywhere we were well received.

Over a century previously, a French doctor, Maurice Tamisier, who was serving with the invading Egyptian army led by Mohammed Ali, had described the lands as 'a jewel coveted by all conquerors'. While the title *Arabia Felix* properly belongs to the Yemen, Asir (claimed, in any case, by the Imams of the Yemen as their own) is united with the southern province in enjoying the benefits of sun, water and a fruitful earth.

★　　★　　★　　★

The French historian Fernand Braudel has declared:[12]

> The mountains resist the march of history, with its blessings and burdens, or they
> accept it only with reluctance. And yet life sees to it that there is a constant contact
> between the hill population and the lowlands.

In Arabia there are three zones of high mountain: the northern part of the Hejaz in the region known as Midian; from Taif through Asir and the Yemen to the Gulf of Aden; and in Oman, across the peninsula on the Arabian Gulf. Of the three, the northern mountains are wild, inhospitable, and largely abandoned by man, while the latter two conform closely to Braudel's hypothesis. Southern Arabia stretches from the peaks of the Yemen, through the lowlands of Aden and the valleys of the Hadramaut, via the Omani province of Dhofar to the mountains of Oman proper. Mountains form one barrier: the great desert of the Rub' al-Khali which lies behind the coastal zone provides another and the society which has developed under their protection differs markedly from that to the north.

Bertram Thomas, who in 1931 was the first European to cross the Empty Quarter – The Rub' al-Khali – described the south thus:[13]

> Arabia Felix! Strange that the epithet 'Happy' should grace a part of the earth's surface, most of it barren wilderness where, since the dawn of history, man has ever been at war with his environment and his neighbour. Yet there can be no mistaking the classical geographers. To Strabo, Pliny, and Ptolemy, the term Arabia Felix served for the entire peninsula south of the Syrian desert (Arabia Deserta) and the mountains about Sinai (Arabia Petraea). True, the term consorts ill with the horrid wastes of Rub' al-Khali that form no small part of Arabia, but there lies in the central south, bordering the Indian Ocean, a land at once of rare physical loveliness and of ancient fame. If there be any region in Arabia entitled to the epithet 'Happy,' other than the Yemen, whose glories were well known to the ancients, it is this province of Dhufar, an Arcadia of luxuriant forests that clothe steep mountains overlooking the sea, of perennial streams and sunny meadows, of wide vistas and verdant glades. Here, according to the writer of Genesis, Jehovah had set the limit of the known world 'as thou goest east unto Mount Sephar'; hither came the ancient Egyptians for frankincense to embalm their sacred Pharaohs; here, may be, were hewed the pillars of Solomon's Temple, if indeed Dhufar be not the site of Ophir itself, and the traditional market for ivory and peacocks' feathers.

Man, however, had marred this paradise; the lands of the south became synonymous with political feuds and *vendetta*. One such struggle between the Hinawi and Ghafari factions began in the eighteenth century and has lasted with barely diminished force until recent times. Their struggle echoes the rabid hatred which the Guelfs held for the Ghibellines in medieval Europe, except that the loathing of Hinawi for Ghafari produced more acts of senseless malice. In the Yemen and throughout southern Arabia, this climate of lawlessness made it necessary for towns and villages to be well protected. Shibam, deep in the Wadi Hadramaut, is as much a masterpiece of defensive engineering as of town building; its mud-brick walls and houses built into the fortified perimeter dominate the land around.

Nowhere else in Arabia are the physical contrasts of the landscape so closely juxtaposed. The mountains of the Yemen to the west and Oman to the east rise to over 10,000 feet, while the Wadis of the Hadramaut, like deep cuts gouged into the surface of the earth, are only a little above sea-level although they lie deep inland. Beyond is the desert, perhaps the only part of Arabia which can truthfully be termed '*Forsaken* and *Desolate*'. Wilfred Thesiger was the first man to record the crossing of Uruq al-Shaiba, the 'mountain of sand':[14]

> We were faced by a range as high as, perhaps even higher than, the range we had crossed the day before, but here the peaks were steeper and more pronounced, rising in many cases to great pinnacles, down which the flowing ridges swept like draperies. These sands, paler coloured than those we had crossed, were very soft, cascading round our feet as the camels struggled up the slopes. . . .
> We led the trembling, hesitating animals upward along great sweeping ridges where the knife-edged crests crumbled beneath our feet. Although it was killing work, my companions were always gentle and infinitely patient. The sun was scorching hot and I felt empty, sick, and dizzy. As I struggled up the slope, knee-deep in shifting sand, my heart thumped wildly and my thirst grew worse. I found it difficult to swallow; even my ears felt blocked, and yet I knew that it would be many intolerable hours before I could drink. . . .
> On the summit were no gently undulating downs such as we had met the day before. Instead, three smaller dune-chains rode upon its back, and beyond them the sand fell away to a salt-flat in another great empty trough between the mountains. The range on the far side seemed even higher than the one on which we stood, and behind it were others. I looked round, seeking instinctively for some escape. There was no limit to my vision. Somewhere in the ultimate distance the sands merged into the sky, but in that infinity of space I could see no living thing, not even a withered plant to give me hope. 'There is nowhere to go', I thought.

On the southern coast lay another world. Mukalla, some 200 miles away, looked to India, Africa, and the Gulf ports rather than to the hinterland: before the First World War, it was noted as exporting 'gums, hides, senna and a small quantity of coffee'; imports included 'cotton stuffs, metals and crockery from Bombay, dates and dried fruits from Muscat, and sheep, aloes and frankincense from African ports.'[15]

★   ★   ★   ★

Yet, despite these contrasts in terrain and patterns of life, southern Arabia formed an entity. The tribesmen roamed from the Yemen to Oman, and even through The Sands to the ports of the Arabian Gulf. The Sultan of Oman looked upon Dhofar as a jewel among his possessions, and Sultan Said ibn Timur preferred his palace in Salala to life in Muscat. The interior of Oman had much in common with the Yemen. It shared a reputation for both religious heterodoxy and resistance to central authority. The similarity is more than coincidental; the Ibahdi sect which dominates the mountain regions of Oman had found its staunchest converts in those tribes which claimed descent from a folk-hero, Malik ibn Fahm, Yemeni by birth, who had trekked across southern Arabia with his followers in the third century AD. The Zeidi schismatics, who controlled the central highlands of the Yemen with their capital at Sadah, had little in common doctrinally with the Ibahdis to the east; but geography had provided both with a fastness from which they could fend off invading armies. For some seventy-five years, after their occupation in 1840 (despite an army of more than 30,000 men) the Turks could do no more in the Yemen than control the coastal towns and a few inland centres. Even this minimal occupation produced a series of risings, notably in 1891 and 1904. Contemporary Sultans of Muscat had no modern military force to make their rule effective in the hinterland of Oman and, consequently, the Ibahdi warriors made regular forays down to the coast; in 1895, the Sultan Faisal ibn Turki lost the town of Muscat and was forced to retreat for a time into one of the forts guarding the harbour. The instability of Omani politics was legendary.

Outside the kingdom, the Wahhabis of central Arabia looked upon the Omanis as heretics ripe for conquest and made regular incursions. The only stable force in the region was British imperialism, and the sultans could, in general, rely on British support in moments of crisis. In 1915 a force of 700 Indian soldiers was sent to protect the young Sultan Timur from the advancing Ibahdis. Disciplined firepower dealt the tribesmen a sharp defeat at Beit al-Falaj on the road to Muttrah and Muscat and, with the assistance of a British Political Adviser, a treaty was patched up. However, it could do little more than recognize the *status quo*, and the sultan remained powerless over a large part of his notional domain. Indeed Sultan Said ibn Timur, who succeeded his father Timur in 1932, never visited the towns and villages of the central mountains until 1954, when he drove in some haste from Salala (far to the south in Dhofar) to Muscat.

However, the prize of the sultanate was not the mountain redoubt of the Jebel Akhdar, but the coastal strip known as the Batina, Bertram Thomas, who became famous as the first European to cross the Empty Quarter, was appointed Financial Adviser by Sultan Timur in 1924. One of his duties was to accompany the Sultan on his progresses, and he described the Batina as he saw it from the back of his camel, Khuwara:[16]

Climbing to the top of a lofty sand-ridge ahead, whence the far side slopes down to the sea, we were rewarded with a panorama of much interest. Behind and to the right is the great dark serpentine mass that raises its jagged cliffs about Muscat and for seven miles beyond to Yiti. To the northward stretches away the noble but paler limestone range of the Hajar in a gentle curving sweep. Starting here at the coast, the Hajar range swings gradually in to a maximum distance of forty miles at a point about seventy-five miles north, and thence bends symmetrically back to strike the coast again at Khutma Malaha. Thus enclosed between it and the waters of the gulf of Oman is a crescent plain, the Batinah, the chief province of the Sultanate of Muscat to-day.

A uniform threefold nature characterises the Batinah throughout its great length. First, a stretch of shining sandy beach, very gently shelving and almost everywhere innocent of rocks; secondly, a mighty palm-grove, one of the three largest in the world, which marches with the beach continuously for a hundred and fifty miles, in places two or three miles deep; and thirdly, a great wilderness of shingle plain that stretches back from the palm-grove to the mountains, a plain often skirted with acacia jungle where it meets the palm, and elsewhere largely covered with camel scrub. This plain is the sun-scorched haunt of gazelle.

Water lay close to the surface in the Batina, which facilitated the 'rank luxuriance' which he described. Elsewhere in Oman an elaborate system of irrigation, called *falajes* (which had first been dug by the Persians), were carefully preserved and made possible a relatively flourishing agriculture. But from the tip of the Oman peninsula along the coast of the Arabian Gulf, the picture changes. The settlements are sparse, and cultivation rudimentary. The coastline between Oman and the Qatar peninsula was known as The Pirate Coast: but once the European maritime powers had determined to impose their control on the Gulf, piracy and the slave trade were extirpated. The rulers of the Gulf states were forced back on pearling, fishing and trade as their only means of support: Britain provided *Pax Britannica*, political officers, and commerce, but sought to avoid deeper entanglements in an area which fell, theoretically, within the Turkish sphere of influence. Some states, notably Kuwait under the capable Sheikh, Mubarak al-Sabah, used British influence to counteract Turkish power by signing a treaty with Britain in 1899, and accepting a Political Agent, Captain S. G. Knox, in 1904. Treaties had also been signed with the Sheiks of Abu Dhabi, Dubai, Sharjah, Ajman and Umm al-Qaiwan in 1853 and 1892, giving the British a preponderant influence in the Gulf.[17]

The one verdant patch on an arid and barren coast was the Bahrein archipelago, which like the oases of Hofuf and Qatif on the mainland was fed by underground streams. Water bubbled up to form pools of water on the islands. The main port of Manamah was a major centre of trade, which totalled over £4 million in the years 1911–14; almost all the exports were of pearls, for which Bahrein was the major market in the Arabian Gulf. Like Kuwait, Bahrein was cosmopolitan with a large Indian population and Arabs from all parts of the diaspora, as well as the Gulf and central Arabia. More than half of Bahrein's trade before the First World War was with India and the economic dependence of Kuwait was even greater. It was by indirect means – commerce and advice, rather than by force – that the British hegemony was enforced.

★　　★　　★　　★

The 'Heart of Arabia', as St John Philby described it, was the huge central steppe of Nejd and the highlands of Jebel Shammar. From these regions have come the political forces which for two centuries have determined the fate of the coastal provinces. The doctrine of the holy war – *jihad* – had provided the justification for the centuries of conflict between an expanding Islam and the world outside. Within the framework of Islamic society lay the 'domain of peace'; outside, the 'domain of war'. In the hands of Mohammed ibn Abdul al-Wahhab, a rigorous Muslim puritan, born at Uyaina north of Riyadh in AD 1705 (AH 1115), the concept of the holy war was turned inwards upon those Muslims whose observance was held to be lax or impure. The most notable convert to this ascetic doctrine was the head of the Saud clans, with their capital at Diriyyah and later at Riyadh. The conversion of Ibn Saud took place in 1747, and he married the daughter of Abdul Wahhab: thereafter the fortunes of the Saud clans became committed in a ceaseless struggle to strike down heresy wherever it could be found. In campaign after campaign, for a period of some sixty years, the Wahhabi armies carried fire and the sword into all the populated areas of Arabia, save the high mountains or the lands south of the Empty Quarter. In 1802–5 the Wahhabi armies captured the holy cities of the Hejaz, massacring those who would not accept purification. The fanatical zeal of these servants of God altered little with the passage of time. The Wahhabi warriors of the twentieth century, the *Ikhwan*, were driven by the same unswerving compulsion as their antecedents. Sheikh Hafiz Wahba, an Egyptian who served Ibn Saud as minister and, later, as ambassador in London, recalled the reaction of the Wahhabis to Kuwait after the ascetic life of the desert:[18]

The following story will illustrate the excesses of which the Ikhwan could be capable. During the Battle of Jahra, they declared that all who surrendered would be spared. A few Kuwaiti citizens who thought of taking them literally were warned by fellow-townsmen that it was a trap, but two of them disregarded the warning and surrendered.

The Ikhwan at once put them through a stiff religious examination. The first man was asked what were the essentials of Islam, what were the prayers and when must they be said, and so on, all of which he answered correctly. The Ikhwan then announced that if he knew so much and had still stayed on in Kuwait, when he could have gone to an abode of True Islam (the hijrahs, that is) his conduct was worthy of death; the sentence was carried out forthwith. They then turned to his companion, and began putting him through his paces in his turn. Having seen what had happened, this one decided to take the line of complete ignorance as an excuse for staying in Kuwait, even going so far as to answer the question, 'What is the Koran?' with the answer 'A book printed in Bombay.' The Ikhwan then declared that they had never met such a hopelessly ignorant and godless man in their lives, and summarily executed him as well.

If a member of the Ikhwan met a man wearing a long moustache, he would at once stop him and explain that to grow such a long moustache was to depart from the custom of Mohammed, who wore his own moustache closely clipped. He would urge him to follow the Prophet's example, and, as assistance would place his hand on the offending moustache and bite off the excess. If the man was passing through a hijrah at the time this operation would be performed without any preliminary remonstrance or advice. Anyone seen wearing long robes had them forcibly reduced at once to modest proportions, the pretext being a saying of the Prophet to the effect that 'the superfluous part of a man's dress is doomed to hell'.

Central Arabia was, therefore, an inhospitable place for those many Muslims who did not follow the Wahhabi rule; for the Christian it was virtually *terra incognita*. The number of Europeans who had travelled widely in Nejd before the First World War numbered no more than four, and the claims of one of them – William Gifford Palgrave – are somewhat suspect. Their journeys were made more perilous by wars which lasted, intermittently, for over a century. The capture of Mecca was an affront to the theoretical sovereign of Arabia, the Turkish Sultan, Mahmud II. He was determined to destroy the seemingly irresistible Wahhabi armies, and in 1811 the Pasha of Egypt, Mohammed Ali, reconquered the Hejaz and the Holy Cities: in 1818 his army crossed into the central steppe and destroyed the Saudi capital at Diriyyah. But while the head of the house of Saud was executed in Constantinople and many of his kinsmen imprisoned, the Wahhabi hydra could not be so easily exterminated. New leaders came forward and the Egyptian armies were forced to divert from their attempted conquest of Asir to mount another punitive expedition in 1838. Yet no foreign power could hope to maintain effective control over so large and hostile a territory and in 1841 the Egyptians accepted the inevitable and withdrew their governor from Nejd.

The success of the Sauds, by now established in Riyadh, was overshadowed by the growth of a rival they had themselves nurtured. The *heart of Arabia* was not a single entity, but divided by geography into the stony plateau, of which Riyadh is the chief town, and the highlands (dominated by the ridges of the Jebel Aja and Jebel Selmah) which look to Hail as their capital. In between the two regions lay the province of Qasim, with its rich towns of Boreidah and Anaiza. The Emirate of the North (Jebel Shammar) was a gift from the Imam of Nejd, Faisal ibn Saud, to Abdallah ibn Rashid in gratitude for his support against the foreign invaders; within a generation the Rashids had supplanted the Sauds as the main power in central Arabia.

The rule of both Sauds and Rashids throughout the latter part of the nineteenth century was fragile, dependent on a chieftain's ability to hold together a confederacy of tribes. The first Sauds had been men of great force and energy; when their successors fell to quarrelling among themselves, power passed to the great Rashidi chief, Mohammed ibn Rashid. Doughty, who visited Hail in 1877, described how he had come to power 'with a blade into his nephew's bowels', the same nephew who had murdered Mohammed's brother and thereby taken the Emirate. He had established himself in his capital in the manner of a Turkish sultan:[19]

'Hearken, all of you! Rashidy has slain a Rashidy – there is no word for any of you to say! let no man raise his voice or make stir, upon pain of my hewing off his head wellah with this sword.'

In Hayil there was a long silence, the subject people shrunk in from the streets to their houses! Bedouins in the town were aghast, inhabitants of the khala, to which no man 'may set doors and bars', seeing the gates of Hayil to be shut round about them.

An horrible slaughter was begun in the Kasr, for Mohammed commanded that all the children of Telal should be put to death, and the four children of his own sister, Mohammed's own mother. Their uncle's bloody command was fulfilled, and the bleeding warm corpses, deceived of their young lives, were carried out the same hour to the burial; there died with them also the slaves, their equals in age, brought up in their fathers' households, their servile brethren that else would be, at any time, willing instruments to avenge them.

Mohammed ibn Rashid reached his zenith in 1887 when he moved south to take control of Riyadh from the failing hands of the Saudi emir, whom he dispatched into exile. It would perhaps have been more prudent to have adopted the same draconian measures he had used against his own family, as Doughty described, and put the Sauds to the sword. For, within five years of his death in 1897, a Saud had retaken Riyadh by force of arms, and the family of Rashid were deep in the fratricidal slaughter which had so weakened the Saudi family a generation before and allowed the Rashids to take power.

With the shift of authority once again from Hail to Riyadh, central Arabia entered a new phase. Its significance was almost entirely misunderstood. The author of *The Penetration of Arabia* (1904), and the greatest authority on Arabia of his day, D. G. Hogarth, remarked to St John Philby shortly after the young man's epic crossing of Arabia from the Gulf to the Red Sea:[20]

> 'All you say, Philby, about Ibn Sa'ud,' he said one day, 'may be perfectly correct. He may well be the big man you represent him to be; and he certainly has achieved quite astonishing results in pacifying and organizing the warring tribes of Arabia. But after all what is he? A great Badawin chief of outstanding ability like the old Muhammad ibn Rashid and others who have passed across the Arabian stage, leaving their mark on history certainly, but nothing like a permanent organization. We know what has invariably happened on their deaths – a wild reversion to the natural chaos and anarchy of Arabia.'

That Hogarth was wrong, and with him, the British Foreign Office, is easy to explain. To the distant observer, Ibn Saud seemed merely another able desert chieftain; of those who had come to know him, the first, Captain W. G. Shakespear was killed fighting for the Emir of Nejd, Abdul-Aziz ibn Abdul-Rahman al-Saud, in 1915, and the second, St John Philby, was so prickly and intractable that his views tended to be discounted in political and diplomatic circles. Ibn Saud's military talents were dismissed, as was his creation of a permanent and stable military force, by forming settlements for his most fanatical warriors – the *Ikhwan* or Brotherhood. By this means he was able to gather an army from a settled population more reliable, and more accessible, than the wandering nomads who largely made up the battle camp of the Rashids. He had a clear strategic vision, as when he recaptured the coastal province of Hasa, which the Turks had taken from the enfeebled Saudis in 1871. He seized Hofuf, the capital of Hasa, in 1913 with virtually no resistance, for the Turks, as he knew, had been busily engaged in the Balkan wars and were in no condition to fight. Thereafter he enlarged his territories piecemeal: Jebel Shammar fell in 1921 and in the last week of August 1924 the Wahhabi armies were loosed on the Hejaz.

Taif fell to them in an orgy of bloodshed, which was far from Ibn Saud's intention. Mecca was occupied on 13 October, but Jiddah held out against the Saudis until December 1925; a month later, Ibn Saud was proclaimed King of the Nejd and Hejaz. Later in 1926, he extended his protection to Asir against encroachments from the Yemen. Although there have been numerous border incidents with the states which surrounded the new kingdom, in the years since the proclamation of the Kingdom of Saudi Arabia in 1932, its boundaries have remained stable. Ibn Saud brought peace to the heart of Arabia, a peace which reached even to remote and warring tribes. He was the most successful ruler both in war and peace in the modern history of Arabia, and the father not only of his country but also of a new sense of Arabian identity.

The chronological boundaries of this book, from the mid-1880s to the beginning of the 1950s, are artificial in that they begin with the first surviving photographs of the region and end not with the first exploitation of oil, but as its true importance for Arabia becomes clear. It describes a society which is moving from poverty to great wealth. Many things portrayed in these pages have vanished, like the walls of Jiddah or the old streets of Riyadh: modernization has blown away the gossamer illusion of *Araby*.[21] But, despite these superficial changes, modern Arabia is removed at most by only three generations from the world as depicted here, and the appreciation of that past and of its values must grow rather than decline with time.

DESERTS

The spirit of the desert dominated Arabia even at points remote from the great stony central plateau or the sandy wastes of the Dahna or the Rub' al-Khali – the Empty Quarter. This sense of superiority, of the desert Arab over the city dwellers of the Hejaz, has its origins in the early days of Islam, for although the first Muslims came from Medina, and latterly Mecca, it was the tribes and confederations of the interior which provided the mainspring of Islamic expansion. The pattern has repeated itself in more recent history, for the powerful Wahhabi movement of puritan Islam, headed by the Saud family of the Nejd, imposed the values of the desert upon the decadent cities. An observer of the Wahhabi conquest of Mecca in 1807 noted with some surprise:

> they never steal neither by force nor by trickery, except when they believe an object to belong to an enemy or an unbeliever; everything they buy and every service rendered them they pay for with their money. Blindly following their leaders, they silently endure every kind of hardship, and will let themselves be led to the ends of the earth.

The complex code of the desert Arabs regulated every aspect of their lives, from the gift of hospitality (even if it meant starvation for the host and his family) to the blood feud and the hallowing of vengeance. The code was based on the simple practical sanction that those who broke it were cast out from their people; an outcast, shunned by all, was doomed. News travelled with amazing speed up and down the peninsula: the first question of any travellers in the desert to those they met on the way was: '*What is the news?*' Thus, despite the huge extent of the peninsula, and the many peoples and terrains which it comprised, it was often impossible to escape an infamous reputation. Survival in the conditions of desert life depended on loyalty and mutual dependence among clansmen.

The desert towns – like Riyadh, Hail, and Hofuf – had little in common with the sophistication of the western cities of Arabia; they were extensions of the desert life, and the capital cities for powerful families, like the

16

Sauds of Riyadh or the Rashids of Hail. Even the ports of the Arabian Gulf –
Kuwait, Muscat, Dubai – which looked to the outside world were also the
trading centres for the men of the desert, who came to buy and sell, and
exchange news. It was from the towns that the great families began, gradually,
to impose their will on the desert dwellers, levying taxes upon them and
forcing the Bedu, where they could, to abandon the old code of desert
vendetta, for the law courts of the *emir*'s judges. The balance of power moved
decisively into the hands of the rulers when, with radio and the motor car
(although the latter was something of a false friend) they held a power of
communication faster than the whispers and rumours of the desert travellers.
Within a few years of Ibn Saud's adoption of radio throughout his realm, the
distant tribes began to acknowledge him as effective overlord. Thereafter, the
life of the desert was doomed.

Bedu tribesman,
south-eastern Arabia,
about 1925

previous spread
Wahhabis at afternoon prayer, in the Wadi al-Shajara,
1917
The Wadi, on the route between the Arabian Gulf and
Riyadh, takes its name from the acacia trees seen here,
the only trees between Hofuf in the Hasa, and the
Turabi valley, a few days march from Riyadh.

top right
Travelling in the territory of the Rashids, north of Hail,
1913

bottom right
In the centre of Arabia: the pilgrim road from Riyadh
to Mecca
The soil of the Shaib Qahqa is a rough black gravel,
which is well covered with coarse grass and low bushes,
which provide grazing for camels. Behind lie the
granite peaks of the Damkh range.

below
Travellers in Arabia, about 1917

The Emir of Nejd and some of his
family, at camp in the desert, 1910
In this photograph the Emir, Abdul-Aziz
ibn Abdul-Rahman al-Saud, the future
King Ibn Saud of Saudi Arabia, is in his
thirty-first year

above
Al-Saleh, the 'great tracker'

top right
A midday halt for coffee in the desert south of Kuwait,
28 November 1909

bottom right
Gertrude Bell's party in camp on their journey to Hail,
1913

The main street of Riyadh, 1914

The approach to Riyadh, 1914
    The city is completely encircled by a thick wall of
coarse sun baked mud bricks, about twenty-five
feet in height and surmounted by a fringe of plain
shark's tooth design; at frequent intervals, its
continuity is interrupted by imposing bastions . . .
and guard turrets.

        (Philby, *Heart of Arabia*, I, 70).
The fort, which was seized by Ibn Saud with a handful
of followers from its Rashidi garrison in 1902, was a
massive building, with bastions at each corner; the royal
palace, of which the towers can be seen in the
photograph, was built by the victorious Sauds.

27

Riyadh: the Suq (market place), 1914
Shakespear noted that almost a third of the town was
taken up by palaces built for the Saud family in the
years since 1902.

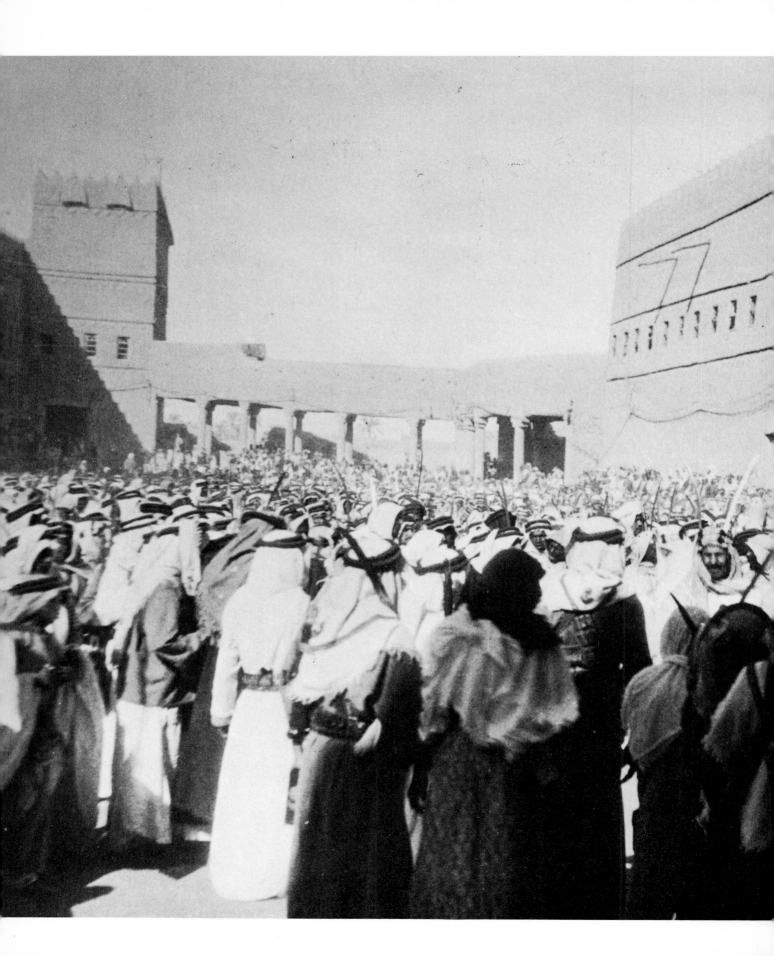

overleaf
left
Travelling in the interior of the Empty
Quarter; the dunes rise to more than 700
feet
right
The great dune barrier of the Urug al
Shaiba

Ibn Saud leading his clansmen in a dance. The tall
figures behind him are members of the Royal Guard

In the Palace at Riyadh, 1912
The white clad figure in the centre is Ibn Saud's
brother.

right
St John Philby, far left, with his camel at
the start of his journey across Arabia, 1917

below
A young boy at Kaf, 1921

On this camel, Philby crossed the Empty Quarter, and then journeyed on to Mecca, 1931. He described her as 'the heroine of the confinement in the desert, the best of all our beasts.'

Philby was narrowly beaten by Bertram Thomas as the first to cross the Empty Quarter; in fact, he took a more difficult route than Thomas had done.

The wells of Hazil, in the territory of the Ruwala, 1912
Doughty described this place laconically as a 'watering place made in the
hollow ground'.

The palace and mosque at Hail, capital of the Rashids, and of the Jebel
Shammar, 1913
Gertrude Bell saw little of Hail, since she was held in comfortable
confinement for most of her stay there. On her last morning she took as
many photographs as she was permitted to, and her description is
impressionistic:

> The battlement ring of mud wall encircles Hail, the line broken at
> regular intervals by ruined towers, battlemented also, machiolated,
> narrowing upwards like wingless windmills . . . Dominating the city,
> the great round towers of the Qasr, the Amir's palace, crown the
> massive defences which guard the secrets and domestic tragedies of the
> Rashid.

Tribesmen of eastern Arabia,
mid-1920s

Bedu of the Bani Kaab tribe,
Oman Peninsula, *c.* 1926

bottom of page
Drawing water in the Wadi Hanifah outside Riyadh, 1914
Barclay Raunkiaer, the first European visitor to Riyadh in this century described the well-head, which surmounted a well almost 80-feet deep, as 'that great wooden engine of fruitfulness, which whines and creaks incessantly while water ripples out in clear streams through the channel.'

far right
Gertrude Bell photographed Ibn Saud at Basra in December 1916
She published her impressions of him in the following month:

> Ibn Saud is now barely forty, though he looks some years older. He is a man of splendid physique, standing well over six feet, and carrying himself with the air of one accustomed to command. Though he is more massively built than the typical nomad sheikh, he has the characteristics of the well-bred Arab, the strongly marked aquiline profile, full-flesh nostrils, prominent lips accentuated by a pointed beard. His hands are fine, with slender fingers . . . [a] slow sweet smile.

right
The high land of Nejd, Jebel Tuwaiq

> North and south ran a long unsteady line of cliffs,
> facing west and rising by a sheer precipice from the
> plain below to the edge of the plateau . . . majestic
> headlands jutted out from this line at intervals into
> the plain, which merged to the westward in a vast
> sea of sand.
>
> (Philby, *Heart of Arabia*, I, 121)

The oasis of Ghubaiya, in the Jabrin district, north-east
of the Empty Quarter. Philby's guide, Suwid, holds a
wounded raven they had found on their journey. Suwid
had himself planted the palms seen here beside a pool.
Jabrin was an *Ikhwan* settlement, and the desert around
held by the Murra tribe

Hofuf. The view over the Suq al Khamis. When Barclay Raunkiaer came here in 1912, he wrote of recently captured robbers and murderers having iron fetters forged onto their limbs: the region of Hofuf was notorious for bandits until they were suppressed by Ibn Jalawi, a kinsman of Ibn Saud

The army of Ibn Saud on the march,
near Thaj in the Hasa, 1911

Ibn Saud at his meeting with Sir Percy Cox, at Uqair
on the coast of the Hasa, 1920

The end of enmity. King Ibn Saud meets King Faisal I of Iraq.
Early 1930s
The hatred of Hashemite for the Saud family which followed the
capture of the Hejaz and the expulsion of the Hashemites, ebbed
away slowly during the 1920s. Both parties realized that they had
more to gain from stability in the region than any temporary
victory on the border could provide. The crisis of the Ikhwan
raids into Iraq in the late-1920s proved to Ibn Saud that
adventurism could threaten the internal stability of his own
regime, and by 1936, relations had so far improved that a treaty
of friendship could be signed between the two countries.

The greatest of the north Arabian tribes, the Ruwala,
seen here in the town of Jauf, captured by their leader,
Nuri es Shaalan; his son, Nuri ibn Shaalan,
photographed here by Captain Shakespear, was the
regent of Jauf. The Ruwala also welcomed the Austrian
scholar, Alois Musil, and his volumes dealing with the
life, customs and society of the tribe have left a vivid
picture of them

The Jebel Tuwaiq, from the south

A halt for coffee on the edge of the northern Nefud
desert, in the land of the Anaiza tribe

Ibn Saud revolutionized the conduct of warfare in the desert. In the first decade of his reign, he created a traditional desert army, comprising his own clan and a fluctuating force of allied tribes. He was not very successful, and experienced the frustration of many battles which ended in stalemate, after a few random fusillades had been fired. He concluded, after the fashion of Oliver Cromwell, that the work 'must be done by the Godly', and he sought to transmute the energies of militant Wahhabism into an effective military force. In 1912, he established the first military settlement or *hijra* at Artawiya, to the north of Riyadh; it was already noted as the home of religious zealots, and he turned their fanaticism to his own ends. The *Ikhwan*, or Brotherhood spread rapidly, and he was able to create some sixty of these settlements, where the Bedu of the desert were transformed into warriors of the True Faith.

As the Ikhwan component of his armies grew, he became progressively more successful; within a few years no other Arab army could stand against him on the battlefield. Had he done no more than this, he would be remembered for his perfection of the traditional camel armies of the desert. But Ibn Saud recognized that modern technology would transform the war in the desert. After the end of the First World War, he sought to import motor vehicles, radio, and, latterly, aircraft; for these innovations he attracted the disgust of the Ikhwan, who wanted no part of the works of the ungodly. But these modern means of communication and transport were the instrument he used to break the power of the Ikhwan as, progressively, their fanaticism led them beyond his control. After a series of incidents, in which they ignored his commands, he packed his troops into motor vehicles, armed them with machine guns, and against the advice of all, sent them north to ambush the Ikhwan, who were returning from one of their raids into Iraq. At the battle of Sibla, the Ikhwan, led by the redoubtable Faisal al-Duwish, were harried by British bombers, and the guns of Ibn Saud's motorized column. The remnants of the Ikhwan turned to raiding and guerrilla war, and a long campaign was needed to destroy them; with their strength destroyed, Ibn Saud was able to declare 'From today we live a new life.'

Ibn Saud possessed, as a military commander, an extraordinary clear-sightedness, and a patience to fashion the instrument he needed to fit his ends. It was a talent which enabled him to move beyond being merely a desert warlord, which Arabia possessed in plenty to being a leader effective in war and in peace.

The army of the Wahhabis on the march, photographed
by Captain Shakespear, near Thaj in the Hasa, 1911
The purpose of these raids was to establish the rule of
the Emir of Nejd over the desert tribes of the east:
Turkish power only covered the towns, oases and their
immediate vicinity.

The army of the faithful: the forces of Ibn Saud, led by
the shock troops of the Ikhwan advance in line of battle,
about 1918

War in the desert
Ibn Saud distributes camels to his fighting men at
Suleimiya about fifty miles south-east of Riyadh.

The experience of modern war: Ibn Saud at Basra, 16 December 1916

Ibn Saud's first journey outside the confines of Arabia was to Basra, where the British sought to impress him with their military might; the lesson of modern armaments was not lost on him. Gertrude Bell, his guide, 'took him in trains and motors, showed him aeroplanes, high explosive, anti-aircraft guns, hospitals, base depots, – everything.' He quickly saw the implications of aviation and later, radio, for desert warfare: this receptivity to military innovation gave him the edge over all his enemies.

Ibn Saud with British officers at Basra

Viewing a bomber

With other Arab leaders

Inspecting Indian cavalry

Ibn Saud and his family at Riyadh, 1918
He is clearly recognizable by his great height. The
young man with long hair is his eldest son Turki,
already a renowned soldier. He died in the great
influenza epidemic of 1918. Ibn Saud's younger sons,
Mohammed and Khalid, and his nephews Faisal, Fahad
and Saud, are standing in front. He used the dynastic
marriage as a deliberate instrument of policy, marrying
and then divorcing wives to stay within the Koranic
limits of four at any one time.

right
King Ibn Saud in later life

Camels at rest, northern Nejd, 1913
'What other creature is as patient as the camel? That is
the quality which endears them to us Arabs.' To the
desert Arab, who can describe a camel's age and origins
merely by looking at its tracks, it provides shelter, with
tents and clothing woven of camel hair, transport, milk,
wealth, and eventually meat. Nothing was wasted, as
Alois Musil discovered in 1909:

> Before five o'clock . . . some women and girls
> came to our camp, each carrying a vessel. As soon
> as we had untied the left forelegs and they had
> risen, the women rushed to them and caught the
> urine in their vessels . . . Some of the smallest girls,
> who had got to the camels last . . . lowered their
> heads under the tails of the camels and let the
> intermittently flowing urine fall all over their
> heads, faces, necks and breasts. Every piece of
> camel dung was collected by the women and
> carried away.
>
> (Alois Musil, *Northern Negd*, 88)

A new age dawns: motor transport in Arabia, 1935
Until 1934, only the Royal House were permitted to
own and use motor cars. Thereafter, they spread
rapidly, advanced considerably by St John Philby, who
negotiated a Ford concession and used motor transport
to explore vast stretches of Arabia. But with the coming
of vehicles, and, later, the building of roads, the old life
of the desert began to die.

A water-hole in the Bani Qitab country, Sharjah
The Bani Qitab were one of the small tribes which
wandered through the desert hinterland of the states of
the Arabian Gulf; they acknowledged the Sheikh of
Umm al-Qaiwan as their overlord, but ranged far and
wide.

The Wadi Iram, the approach to Akaba

Faisal, the most able of Ibn Saud's many sons.
He eventually became the third King of Saudi Arabia,
only to die at the hands of an assassin. 1919

right
            About 1927

THE GATEWAY OF
ARABIA

For the mass of pilgrims who arrived each year at the ports of the Hejaz –
120,000 at Jiddah alone in some years – the coastal towns were merely the
gateway to Mecca, the Mother of Mercy. For non-Muslims, forbidden the
holy cities of Mecca and Medina, Jiddah was their foothold in Arabia. Many of
those who came by sea were illiterate, but the first impressions of one foreigner
are worth recording here:

> We had the accustomed calm run to Jiddah. . . . By day we lay in shadow; and for
> great part of the glorious nights . . . under the stars in the steaming breath of the
> southern wind. But when at last we anchored in the outer harbour, off the white
> town hung between the blazing sky and its reflection in the mirage which swept
> and rolled over the wide lagoon, when the heat of Arabia came out like a drawn
> sword and struck us speechless. . . . There were only lights and shadows, the white
> houses and the black gaps of streets. . . .
>
> We walked past the white masonry of the still-building watergate and
> through the oppressive alley of the food market. . . . In the air, from the men to
> the dates and back to the meat, squadrons of flies like particles of dust danced up
> and down the sunshafts which stabbed into the darkest corners of the booths
> through torn places in the wood and sackcloth awnings overhead. The
> atmosphere was like a bath.
>
> T. E. Lawrence, *Seven Pillars of Wisdom.*

For the most part, the visitor spent as little time as possible in Jiddah,
and took the first camel caravan for Mecca, which meant a journey of some
twenty-three hours on the swaying back of a camel; for those in a hurry, the
Hasawi donkeys covered the distance in half the time.

Awaiting the arrival of the pilgrim ships on Jiddah
quay, 1935
From an album prepared by Dr Oscar Marcus to
commemorate the Haj of 1935.

above
Jiddah from the sea

top right
Small boats were used to trans-ship the pilgrims from the
large ships to the shore, mid-1930s

bottom right
The boatmen of Jiddah, who ferried the pilgrims from
their ships to the shore. The trade was divided between
many guilds, one of which is seen here with their chief,
second from left, early 1880s

71

above and right
Pilgrims arriving on Jiddah quay.
They are wearing the *Ihram*, the
traditional white robe of the
Muslim pilgrim, about 1900

far right
The town crier of Jiddah

Keeping tally of the pilgrims as they arrive. The dues
paid by pilgrims were a major source of income to the
rulers of the Hejaz

Waiting for the caravan to Mecca

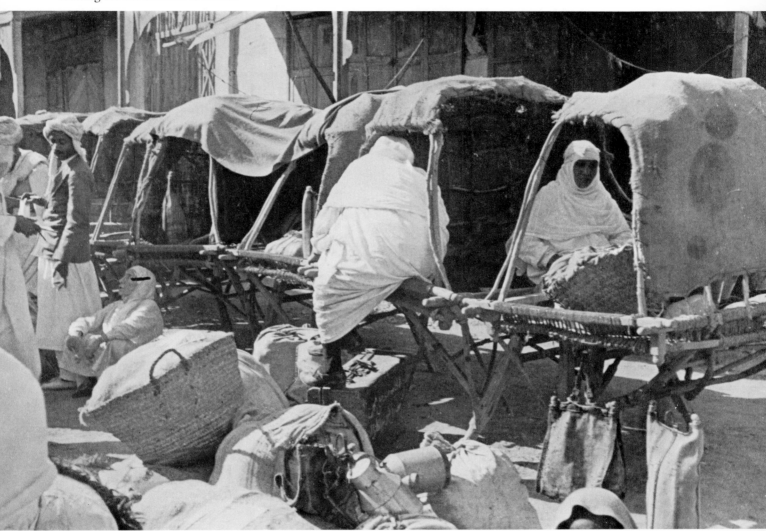

The reputed Tomb of Eve (*Umina Howa*
– Mother of us all) outside the walls of
Jiddah. The grave is supposed to
correspond to the life-size of its
occupant, some 200 yards. The shrine is
venerated by Far Eastern pilgrims, who
have traditionally made it the first duty
of the pilgrimage to pray for her soul,
about 1927

overleaf
The port of Jiddah, the main commercial
centre on the Red Sea coast of Arabia

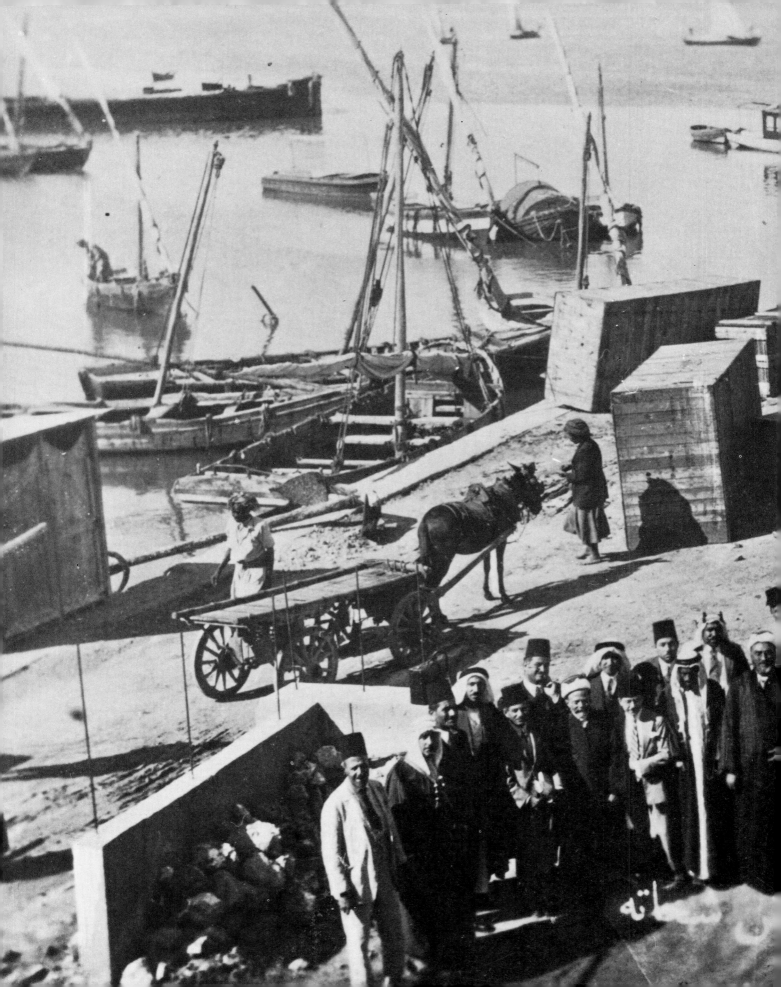

Men of Jiddah, 1934

left
A rich merchant with his Circassian servant, about 1880

A Turkish official, with his son and
servants, early 1880s

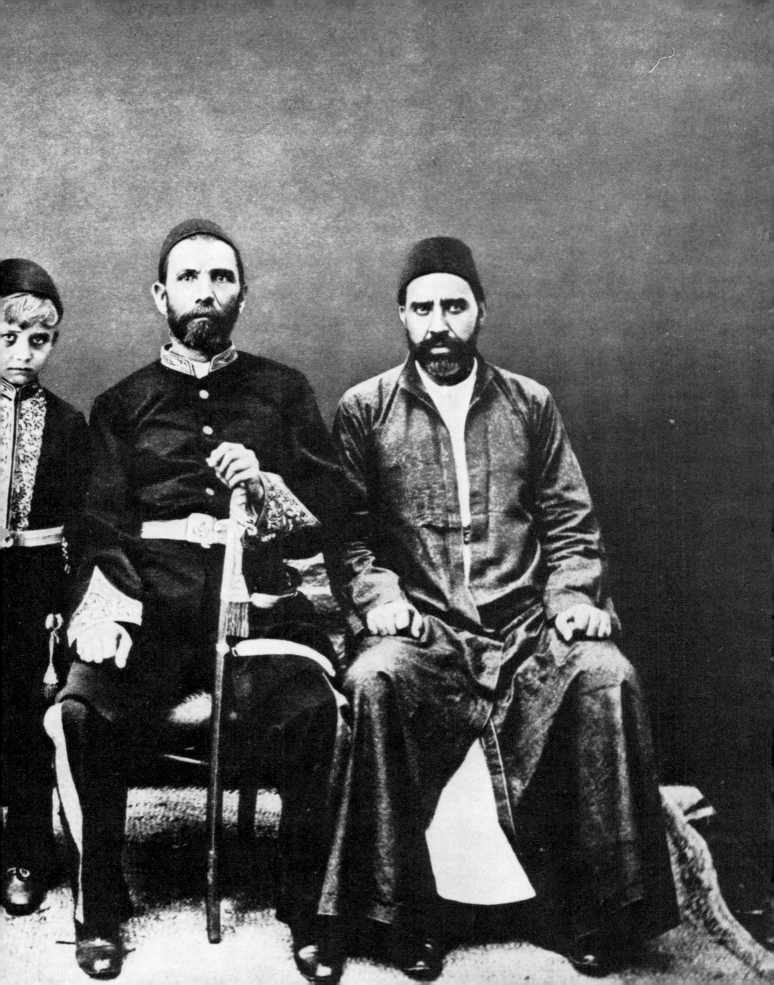

The Customs House

The Mecca Gate in the walls of Jiddah; the walls have
since been demolished

A peddler in Jiddah, about 1885

The streets of Jiddah

Jiddah market-place, looking
north, 1917

right
Market outside the gates of Jiddah, with the traditional
tall houses of the city behind, 1936

bottom right
A potter's shop, about 1936. Many of the finer items for
table were imported, and the local products were crude
and undistinguished

below
Prisoners, 1934. The conditions in Arabian prisons were
primitive, and the dangers of disease were heightened
by the unhealthy climate of the Hejaz coast

91

left

Hejazi, about 1900

The great tribes of the Hejaz are the Harb, the Oteiba, who were both nomadic, and the clans of the Ashraf, who claimed descent from Hasan, a grandson of the Prophet. The latter provided the ruling caste of the region.

below

The troops of Midian: a gathering of the sheikhs of the great northern tribes – the Beni Sakhr, the El Fakir, the Ruwala, the Wulid Ali, the Howeitat – under Turkish auspices, 1909

The tribes of the north were powerful, anarchic, and usually at feud with each other. The Turkish interest lay in protecting travellers, and especially the Hejaz railway from their depredations. By bribery and other pressures, they created a temporary peace. But the north – the lands of Midian and the desert to the east – were some of the most dangerous parts of Arabia.

top left

The place near Zeima, with 'menzil trees and the
shadows of rocks', where Charles Doughty was
captured and threatened with death. It was photographed
by the British envoy, Sir Andrew Ryan, on his journey
to Riyadh in November 1935

bottom left

The Wadi Fatima, the first sign of civilization for the
desert traveller. Hadda was 'a large grove of palms with
a few stone huts, an imposing mosque, and a few poor
shops'

above

On the road from central Arabia to the Red Sea: the
Wadi Haradh, 'a sandy valley varying from 50 to 400
yards in width and bordered by hills rising to 300 and
400 feet on either side'.
(Philby, *The Heart of Arabia*, I, p. 210)

left and above

Midian, to the north of the Hejaz, is rocky and waterless. Along the shore line are a few towns, like Muweilah and Dhaba, which were garrisoned by the Turks; inland, settlements were made along the line of the Hejaz railway and a natural oasis at Tebuk

right

Akaba, the gateway to Arabia, was the first great victory of the Arabs over the Turks during the First World War. The town lies on the eastern shore of the Gulf of Akaba, with a small square Turkish fort, a telegraph office, and a few houses. The Bedu, led by T. E. Lawrence and their chiefs, captured 700 Turkish soldiers and 42 officers:

> Through the whirling dust we perceived that Akaba was all a ruin. Repeated bombardments by French and English warships had degraded the place to its original rubbish. The poor houses stood about in a litter, dirty and contemptible.
>
> (T. E. Lawrence, *The Seven Pillars of Wisdom*)

THE HEART OF ISLAM

The pilgrims have come to the holy cities of Mecca and Medina since the early days of Islam, to walk seven times round the Kaaba in Mecca, and fulfil the other duties of the Haj. Some would follow the journey of the Prophet from Mecca to Medina, and visit the tombs of the second city of Islam. But while the ritual of the pilgrimage followed the same form through the centuries, the holy cities changed with the riches that the pilgrimage brought. By the second half of the nineteenth century, Meccan society was an amalgam of many different races, customs, and bizarre superstitions – all carefully recorded by a Dutch scholar, Christian Snouck Hurgronje. He married a Meccan woman and was apparently accepted within the city at all levels of society. Although other Europeans had penetrated the city in the guise of Moslems, none of them had the depth of Hurgronje's understanding and sympathy for Meccan life:

> I must once again observe: he who sees the Mekkans outside the pilgrimage season (in it they are like business men when on 'change') finds them gay, affable, hospitable to extravagance, entirely devoted to social life, and he who obtains admission into good family circles meets, along with many vulgar creatures, also noble human characters and unfeigned piety.
>
> C. S. Hurgronje, *Mekka*, tr., 1931, p. 10.

The old Mecca portrayed by Hurgronje, and all the extravagant ceremonies which had been added to the pilgrimage, was ended when the Ikhwan occupied the holy cities, and restored them to a Koranic purity.

The Royal car *en route* to the Great Mosque. Late 1930s.
King Ibn Saud held a great reception each year in his
palace at Mecca, to which all the visiting dignitaries, who
were making the pilgrimage, were invited

The land-caravan of pilgrims travelling from
Jiddah to Mecca, 1912

Mecca, set in an arid plain below the hills, 1886

previous spread
The cemetery near Mecca where most of the
Prophet's family are buried, about 1910

A city of tents on the Plain of Arafat, 1912
When Philby made the pilgrimage for the first
time, he noted 'All over the immense plain . . .
it was the lines and phalanxes of camels that
caught my eye. There must have been 50,000
of them at least.'

Pilgrims collecting water, 1912

above
'The streets of Mecca are narrow and irregular,
save with the exception of one which is at
places eight metres wide', about 1930 (Spiro
Bey, *The Moslem Pilgrimage*, p. 34)

left
The Town Hall of Mecca

The Kaaba covered with the Holy Carpet, brought from Egypt in the *Mahmal*. The requirements of the pilgrimage are: (i) To wear the pilgrim's robe, the *Ihram*, (ii) to 'stand' on the Plain of Arafat, (iii) to stone the symbols of the great Devil at Muna, (iv) to complete the *Tawaf*, or walking round the Kaaba seven times. The pilgrims tried to kiss the Black Stone (seen bottom right of the Kaaba). They then struggled to drink from the well of Zemzem, said to have been created miraculously by the Angel Gabriel. All these duties were carried out by a jostling crowd of many thousands: 200,000 made the pilgrimage in some years

The congregation in the Great Mosque of Mecca, on Friday during the
week of the pilgrimage. The Kaaba stands in the centre, draped with
the black cloth, the *Kiswa*, about 1910
The building to the left of the Kaaba is the well-head of the waters of
Zemzem, where some fanatics sought to drown themselves, believing
that they thereby gained entry to Paradise.

Pilgrims came from throughout the Moslem world, and
each nationality had guides attached to them; but the
great bulk of pilgrims were Arabians, coming by camel,
horse, donkey or on foot, 1912

The arrival of the *Mahmal* and its
mounted escort in Mecca, about
1910

Meccan women of the 1880s, dressed for the street
(left), and in the clothes worn at home. Even given the
laxity of Meccan society, it was a remarkable
achievement to take such a photograph

A woman of Mecca. Many writers wrote about the
morals of the Meccans and the temptations of the flesh
which lured the pilgrims from their tasks, 1884

Mecca under Turkish rule. The deputy governor
addresses the leading dignitaries of the city and the
surrounding countryside. The region was heavily
garrisoned, as the profusion of military uniforms
indicates

The Turkish Governor of Mecca,
c. 1885

The prize camel of the Sherif Jahja, with richly decorated harness. Jahja, a younger member of one of the leading Meccan families, is seen here with his personal slave (left), an escort, and camel driver. The escort's rifle is wrapped to prevent damage by sand, a normal precaution, 1886

The Grand Sherif of Mecca, 1882

Servant and eunuch with the child of their master. Most eunuchs, who were imported from Africa in their mutilated state, were employed to keep order in the holy places. Very few were kept by private individuals, making the master of this slave a man of great importance, c. 1886

A Meccan bride upon her wedding day, weighed down by the traditional costume. The coins and jewels which she wears are evidence of the wealth and standing of her family. As Hurgronje noted of one wedding: 'she is hardly able to sit down, though propped from behind by silk cushions. Her hands are raised aloft and her feet stretched out. She looks like a formless mass, her face and figure hardly distinguishable, a moveable exhibition of jewellery and costly stuff.'

A Meccan bridegroom, seated upon the bridal 'throne',
early 1880s

The inauguration of the Hejaz Railway, 3 October
1908. Between Damascus and Medina there were
seventy-five stations, and the trains never went faster
than nineteen miles per hour; half that was a more
normal speed

right
The main street of Medina, the second holy city of Islam;
the street leads from the great mosque to the tomb of
the Prophet

The Prophet's tomb in Medina and the gardens
of Sayyida Fatima, about 1909

127

above
The interior of the mosque at Medina, 1909

top left
The market-place of Medina, 1908

bottom left
View over Medina: the minarets indicate the tomb of
the Prophet, about 1904

ARABIE
THE BLEST

Writers, ancient and modern, have vied with each other to distil the qualities of southern Arabia. Poets have held to the image of Ophir, the land of frankincense – Milton's '*spicie shoare*'. Others have claimed it as the original home of the Arab people, who spread northwards and eastwards over the peninsula, *Arab al-Araba*. But only those who have experienced the life and people of southern Arabia can express the essence of the region. Freya Stark, who lived among the people of the Hadramaut, once wrote:

> In all places where men have lived for long the marks of their sojourn must linger, but most often, visited by successive tides, they are altered or buried under many oblivions. In South Arabia, nothing much has come to change them through the centuries, except the natural and little-destructive forces of decay.
>
> *Seen in the Hadhramaut*, London, 1938, pp. xxii–xxiii.

Houses at Sana, capital of the Yemen, 1912

Children from the poorer classes at Sana, going to fetch
water. There were wells both inside and outside the
walls. The old town, which included the crowded
quarter where the poor congregated, was surrounded
by a massive wall, repaired at great cost by the Turks

In the house of the Mayor of Sana, 1912. The
pipes grouped in the centre are indicative of
the relaxed attitude towards tobacco held by
the Zeidis. The guests are wearing the white
turbans and silk robes of the well-to-do

A bookshop at Sana. The large white turban
was universally worn by those who had
pretensions to learning, 1912

The Imam Ahmed, while still Crown Prince, at Taiz,
1947
The Zeidi Imamate was founded in the tenth century,
but its power came with an energetic Imam, Qasim, in
the seventeenth. The Imams had become a by-word for
corruption and incompetence, and their power was
bitterly resented by much of the population in the
south; the Zeidi strongholds were in the north, and the
Turks dominated the coastline.

In the high mountains north of Ibb: two young girls at
El Hadeida. At the time of the photograph, they were
about fourteen, and had been married at about the age
of twelve; they were married to men of fifty to sixty

Traditional medicine in the Yemen: cupping with horns
and leeches, pre-1914

A slave making bread at El Tanem, in the Tihama, 1912

The market-place at Badjil, in the highlands of
Yemen

Tribesmen from the Hajar, the mountains which
dominated the coastline of Oman to the promontory of
Ras al-Hadd. The peoples of the interior were fiercely
independent, recognizing only the authority of their
own leaders and disdainful of the coastal tribes

A mountain warrior

Bedu tribesman from south Arabia

Shehari boy in the Qara mountains of Dhofar, southern
Arabia

THE HORN OF PLENTY

'Is this Arabia,' wrote James Wellsted as he climbed into the highlands of the Jebel Akhdar late in December 1835, 'this the country we have looked on heretofore as a desert?' His reaction echoed that of many desert travellers who came upon Oman, and found there a cornucopia. Wellsted described: 'Verdant fields of grain and sugarcane, stretching along for miles, are before us; streams of water, flowing in all directions, intersect our path.' On the coast of Muscat, the same plenty could be found: the great groves of date palms stretched along the shoreline of the Batina from the capital in the direction of the rocky tip of the horn, Ras Musandam. The vast area of Muscat and Oman contained, in addition to the bountiful lands, great tracts of bare rock and desert, as Wellsted found later in his travels:

> From the summit of the Jebel Akhdar I had an opportunity during a clear day to obtain an extensive view of the desert to the southwest of Oman. Vast plains of loose drift, across which even the hardy Bedouin scarcely dares to venture, spread out as far as the eye can reach. Not even a hill nor even a change of colouring in the plains occurs to break the unvarying and desolate appearance of the scene.

But the overall impression of the region remains that of *plenty* rather than *desolation*.

Women walking along the shore of the Batina,
with the famous date groves in the
background, *c.* 1924

Date palms outside Muscat

Muscat harbour, about 1890

Sultan Timur ibn Faisal al bu Said and his advisers, 1919

The watch-tower in the Wadi Jizzi, guarding
the Batina from the tribes of the interior

Bertram Thomas and his camel, Khuwara

below
The Wali of Boshar and his retainers, mid-1920s

top right
Men at prayer, Muscat, about 1930

bottom right
The camels of the Batina are prized throughout Arabia
for their speed and easy stride. But they are pampered
beasts, hand-fed on dates. In the interior of Oman, the
Wahiba own a hardier breed, called 'The Daughters of
Joy', and the Duru, who live between the Jebel Akhdar
and The Sands, cherish the 'Daughters of the Red One'.
Generally, white camels are most desirable, but the
Murra owned a famous prize herd of black camels

left and right
Musicians in Muscat. The strict Ibahdis
discouraged music as sinful; the drum and horn
are traditionally used to accompany dances

below
A village in the Hajar range, Oman peninsula

156

Shihuhite tribesmen of the Ras Musandam peninsula, and dignitaries from Muscat, mid-1920s
The Shihuhites, an ancient pre-Arabian people, lived mostly on fish in the coastal communities; inland they kept great herds of goats.

Sultan Timur of Muscat, 1926
Sultan Timur chose Bertram Thomas to handle his finances, not altogether a happy choice, since Thomas chafed at the demands of business, and sought to make his name as an explorer. Sir Arnold Wilson, who took this photograph, declared that Thomas had 'gained the entire confidence both of the Sultan . . . and of the Council of State.'

Bedu tribesman slaughtering a goat, Oman, 1925

Cairns of this type are common in the Oman Peninsula, and appear in vast numbers. They were about twelve feet in diameter, with a narrow chamber inside – the remains of a pre-Arabian culture. Because of their proximity to the Gulf, Muscat and Oman were often controlled by the Persian empires across the water. The main Persian contribution was in the *falajes* or irrigation system which is still in use today

Ibahdi tribesman,
from central Oman

THE GULF

Sailors from the Gulf were trading with India and China when European sailors were reluctant to venture far beyond their native shores and the traffic in the goods of the East to the markets of the West went on through the ports of the Gulf over the centuries with few interruptions. Yet the wealth which passed through the hands of the Gulf traders over the centuries did little to enrich the population: only pearling in the waters of the Gulf itself provided much employment, with an annual influx from all over Arabia to fill the pearling boats during the season.

During the 1930s, as the pearling industry declined when the market for luxuries shrank with the world recession, geologists discovered that the geological structure of the Gulf region made it a possible source of oil. So little serious interest was shown in the potential of the region that many concessions for exploration and production found no takers in the City of London. Only the earnest advocacy of an American mining engineer Karl S. Twitchell, and his millionaire patron, Charles Crane, persuaded the Standard Oil Company to invest in the region. Few gambles have shown such a spectacular return, and the discovery of other reserves, not only in the Hasa province of Saudi Arabia, but also in the Emirates, in Kuwait, and in Oman, have produced a revolution in the pattern of life which is beginning to get underway as this book closes.

below
A Bedu camp in the hinterland of Abu Dhabi

overleaf
Kuwait water-boats for sale, mid-1930s

Captain Shakespear's Bedu escort in the Kuwait
hinterland, 1909

Women of the Bani Qitab tribe in Sharjah, 1924. They
are wearing the face-mask common in the eastern Gulf

The *majlis* or public audience held by the sheikh in the desert at Sirra, south of Kuwait. Any tribesman could have access to his ruler in the *majlis*, and foreigners found in this tradition the clearest evidence of the natural democracy of the desert Arabs

The meeting of Sheikh Mubarak of Kuwait and Ibn
Saud, Emir of Nejd, March 1910. Mubarak, seated in
the centre, had given sanctuary to the Saud family
when Riyadh was captured by the Rashids in 1892: Ibn
Saud had great respect for the astute Sheikh of Kuwait.
Shakespear met Ibn Saud for the first time and
described him as: 'now in his 31st year, is fair,
handsome and considerably above average Arab height
. . . He has a frank, open face, and after initial reserve, is
of genial and courteous manner.'

Racing at Kuwait, late-1920s

At the end of the First World War, the British wished to express their gratitude to the Sheikh of Kuwait and the Emir of Nejd for their benevolent neutrality. The son of Sheikh Mubarak, Ahmed ibn Jabir, and a younger son of Ibn Saud, Prince Faisal, were taken on a jaunt to England aboard HMT *Kigoma*, where they visited the sights, including London Zoo and an arms factory. They were accompanied by St John Philby, who took his charges to Wales and Ireland, and to Europe for a grand tour of the battlefields. The visit took place against a background of great uncertainty as to the Allies' attitude towards Arabia.

below
The party at London Zoo

right
Sheikh Jabir al-Sabah

far right
Prince Faisal ibn Saud

Sheikh ibn Jabir al-Sabah of Kuwait, with the British
resident, H. Bowman, 1919. The Sheikh died in
mysterious circumstances in 1922, and was succeeded by
his brother Salim

left
Sultan Timur on a naval visit during a tour of the British Isles, accompanied by Bertram Thomas. The British navy had featured prominently in the Gulf, the visible support of the Political Agents and advisers ashore. They came to suppress piracy early in the nineteenth century, stayed to keep down the slave trade, and were, by the last quarter of the century, the controlling power of the region

below
On the tip of Oman, the Ras Musandam peninsula: the Sultan with coastal tribesmen. By virtue of its position, since the narrow straits of Hormuz control the Gulf, Oman was a dominant force in the Arabian Gulf when the power of Persia was in decline

previous spread
Traders on the beach at Kuwait, 1909

right
Watermen on Bahrein Island

below
Bahrein: the al-Khalifa family. Sheikh Hamad ibn Isa al-Khalifa sits in the centre, with Sir Trenchard Fowle on his right and Col. Loch of the Binns on his left. The al-Khalifa clan arrived on the Gulf in 1766, and took possession of Bahrein in 1782–3; the wealth of Bahrein was built on trade and pearling. The first British Political Agent arrived in 1902, but British support did little to mitigate the hardships produced by the collapse of the pearl trade in the 1930s

above
Number Three well at Damman, spring 1935

left
Oil exploration in the Hasa: an Arabian guide tries his
hand at using the alidade

NOTES

This book was completed in the spring of 1979 and in general books published since that date have not been noted.

1 See K. Miller, *Mappa Arabicae*, Stuttgart, 1929. The preliminary brochure is in both English and German.

2 Edward Gibbon, *The History of the Decline and Fall of the Roman Empire*, V, pp. 312–14. The page references are to the standard edition by J. B. Bury, fourth edition, 1911. The whole question of stereotypes of Arabia, and Islam generally is dealt with in spirited fashion in Edward W. Said, *Orientalism*, London, 1978. His conclusions have been critically examined by Richard Luckett in the *Cambridge Quarterly*, vol. 10, no. 3, 1981.

3 Technically speaking a desert is any area with a rainfall of less than 250mm in any year and much of Arabia has less than half this figure. But beyond that narrow and specific sense the word now serves in English as a metaphor of desolation, as in Shelley's *Ozymandias*. The definitions are drawn from the Oxford English Dictionary, and the etymology given there illustrates the extended sense of the word.

4 Lieut. Col. Lewis Pelly, *Report on a Journey to the Wahabee Capital of Riyadh in Central Arabia*, Bombay, 1866. On the topography of Arabia see pp. 19, 22, 26–7, 31, 36, 40.

5 *Ibid.*, p. 43.

6 Wilfred Thesiger, *Arabian Sands*, London, 1959, 1977, p. 128.

7 Alois Musil, *Northern Negd. A Topographical Itinerary*, New York, 1928, p. 317. This volume relates to explorations carried out in 1915. The *Caetani* Musil refers to was Leone Caetani, the author of *L'Arabia preistorica e l'essicamento della terra*, and *L'Arabia e gli Arabi dei tempi storici* (and much else besides), with which Musil took issue.

8 Admiralty Naval Intelligence Division, *A Handbook of Arabia*. vol. 1, London, 1916. This is an extremely useful compilation of information of knowledge concerning Arabia up to the first years of the Great War. Exploration subsequently provided new and better information for areas on which the Handbook is hazy, and it should be used with some caution.

9 Charles M. Doughty, *Travels in Arabia Deserta*, Cambridge, 1888, vol. 1, pp. 5–6. I have used the one volume edition of 1926, to which all references relate.

10 H. St J. B. Philby, *The Heart of Arabia. A record of travel and exploration*, London, 1923, vol. 1, pp. 184, 199–200, 193–4.

11 Wilfred Thesiger, *Arabian Sands*, London, 1959, 1977, p. 17.

12 Fernand Braudel, *The Mediterranean and the Mediterranean World in the Age of Philip II*, London, 1972. Translated from the second French edition, revised 1966, vol. 1, p. 41.

13 Bertram Thomas, *Arabia Felix. Across the Empty Quarter of Arabia*, London, 1932, p. xxiii.

14 Thesiger, *op. cit.*, pp. 148–9.

15 Admiralty, *op. cit.*, pp. 232–3.

16 Bertram Thomas, *Alarms and Excursions in Arabia*, London, 1931, p. 123.

17 The history of British relationships with the Trucial States is covered in Mohammed Morsy Abdullah, *The United Arab Emirates. A Modern History*, London, 1978. The statistics are drawn from the Admiralty Handbook of Arabia, already cited.

18 Sheikh Hafiz Wahba, *Arabian Days*, London, 1964, pp. 130–1.

19 Doughty, *op cit.*, vol. 2, pp. 16–17.

20 H. St J. B. Philby, *Arabian Days. An Autobiography*, London, 1948, pp. 158–9. A list of all Philby's voluminous writings may be found in the excellent biography by Elizabeth Monroe, *Philby of Arabia*, London, 1973.

21 For the *discovery* of Arabia, the classic account is D. G. Hogarth, *The Penetration of Arabia*, London, 1905, written at a time when much of Arabia was still *terra incognita* to Europeans. For the many later travellers, and a general overview of the opening of Arabia to the West, see Robin Bidwell *Travellers in Arabia*, London, 1976.

PICTURE SOURCES

We are grateful to the following for permission to reproduce photographs on the following pages.

Bell Collection, St Antony's College, Oxford: 21, 25, 36, 39, 56, 57, 57, 57, 60, 69
Bowman Collection: 102, 110, 108, 114, 127, 128
Deutsch Collection, Royal Geographical Society: 130, 131, 132, 134, 135, 136, 134, 138
Dickson Collection: 162
Holt Collection: 34
Leachman Collection, Royal Geographical Society: 31, 36
Mansell Collection: 63, 67, 78, 84, 99, 106
Nimmo Collection, St Antony's College, Oxford: 53, 70, 71, 96, 96
Philby Collection, St Antony's College, Oxford: 18, 20, 21, 30, 34, 35, 40, 41, 58, 89, 95, 97, 107

Royal Geographical Society: 93, 129, 137
Rutter Collection: 100, 104, 105, 112, 112, 113
Ryan Collection: 61, 81, 91, 91, 90, 94, 94
St Antony's College, Oxford: 24, 66, 74, 75, 76, 77, 85, 92, 168, 169 170
Shakespear Collection, Major General J. D. Lunt: 26, 26, 28, 38, 44, 48, 49, 50, 64, 164, 174
Shakespear Collection, Royal Geographical Society: 22, 25, 33, 53, 54, 165
Thesiger Collection: 32, 33
Thomas Collection: 17, 37, 37, 62, 140, 139, 141, 143, 150, 151, 152, 153, 154, 155, 156, 157, 158, 159, 161, 164, 173